Carole King

text **Paula Taylor**
illustrations **John Keely**
design concept **Mark Landkamer**

published by **Creative Education**
Mankato, Minnesota

Published by Creative Educational Society, Inc.,
123 South Broad Street, Mankato, Minnesota 56001

Distributed by Childrens Press,
1224 West Van Buren Street, Chicago, Illinois 60607

Library of Congress Number: 75-23185   ISBN: 0-87191-465-4

Library of Congress Cataloging in Publication Data
Taylor, Paula.   Carole King.
1. King, Carole—Juvenile literature.
I. Keely, John.   II. Title.
ML3930.K47T4   784'.092'4   [B]   75-23185   ISBN 0-87191-465-4

Concert in Central Park

The morning of May 25, 1973, dawned grey and cloudy in New York City. But in Central Park, even at that early hour, people were spreading out picnic blankets on the grass. They didn't seem to notice the chilly temperatures and the damp ground; or, if they did notice, they didn't care. That evening, New Yorkers would be turning out in record numbers for a free concert in the park. The early arrivals had decided to wait there all day no matter what the weather. That evening they were determined to be close enough to the stage to see the star of the show — a rock star who is rarely seen, in New York or anywhere, Carole King.

Later that evening, those close to the stage and thousands of not-so-lucky other people would crane their necks to catch a glimpse of the elusive singer. But early that damp morning, the small group of people camped on the lawn could easily see all there was to be seen — workmen assembling scaffolding to hold powerful speakers and amplifiers, painters putting finishing touches on the recently-constructed stage, a few people strolling through the park.

Suddenly, a murmer of excitement rose from the crowd. A tiny, freckle-faced girl in blue jeans had appeared on stage and was walking toward the piano. Her usually long, curly brown hair had been cropped short, but there was no doubting who it was. As Carole sat down at the piano and launched into a few bars of "I Feel the Earth Move," the fans gave her an appreciative round of applause. Carole waved back; But she didn't play long. Apparently satisfied that the sound system was working well, she soon disappeared into a trailer behind the stage.

As the day wore on, the sky grew even more ominously grey. But in spite of the threatened rain, more and more people arrived and sat down on the lawn to wait. Most were high school and college students, but there were older listeners, as well. Carole's music, which she calls "soft rock," appeals to nearly everybody. Her *Tapestry* album has sold over 10,000,000 copies, making it the biggest-selling rock album of all time.

Carole King's Central Park concert promised to be one of the summer's biggest events in New York. Reporters and photographers from major newspapers and television stations began to arrive to cover the concert. They tried to get past security guards surrounding the stage, hoping for an interview with the singer; But Carole remained out of sight. She refused to talk to anyone. Evidently, she'd meant what she said before when asked for interviews. "I want my music to speak for me," she'd insisted. "You can get to know me through my music."

Finally some of the reporters decided that if they couldn't interview Carole, they'd interview her fans, instead. They began wandering through the crowd, asking people why they had come. Some people said they were there because the concert was free. Others said they'd never seen Carole King before and wanted to see her in person; But they all agreed they liked her music. "It's all about the way kids feel today," a young nursing student explained. "She takes people's thoughts, puts them into words, then writes beautiful music for it."

By showtime at dusk, the crowd had swelled to over 70,000. Technicians pleaded with the crowd to stand back from the scaffolding which held the fragile sound equipment. The head of the New York City park department gave a welcoming speech. Finally, Mayor John Lindsay appeared on stage to make the introduction the audience was waiting for. As he finished speaking, Carole King

emerged from a trailer behind the stage. Looking more like a teen-ager than a 34-year-old mother of three, in her blue jeans and plaid madras tunic, she walked quickly across the stage to the piano. As she sat down, Carole turned to the crowd. "It was supposed to rain," she told the audience, with a smile; "but so far, you've been sending out great vibes. Keep it up." Her friendly manner won the crowd over completely. The fans shouted their approval.

Carole smiled back and swung into her first song, "Beautiful." "You've got to get up every morning with a smile on your face/And show the world the love in your heart/Then people gonna treat you better/You're gonna find, yes, you will/That you're beautiful as you feel."

It was a typical Carole King number — the words simple but meaningful, the music lyrical but with a blues feel. Carole writes her songs for her family and friends. Even when she sings them for larger audiences, her music somehow remains intimate. She still seems to be speaking to each person individually as a friend.

Carole herself also remains the same at home or in a concert hall. Onstage or off, she projects the same warmth, honesty and simplicity. She doesn't wear fancy clothes, and she doesn't try to create any kind of stage presence. She sits down and plays for a crowd of 70,000 exactly the same way she would for a group of friends who'd come to her house for an informal jam session.

At the Central Park concert, Carole's fans returned her warmth in full measure. They passed bouquets of flowers to the stage and shouted, "I love you." Some held up signs with song requests. One colorful towel had "We'll Still Love You Tomorrow," painted on it. Noticing it, Carole smiled and responded, "I'll still love you tomorrow, too."

In their enthusiasm, the thousands of fans kept

pressing closer to the stage. In the middle of the concert, the snow fence surrounding the stage collapsed; But Carole seemed not to notice that or other distractions, such as a television camera in a cherry-picker crane which kept swooping down near the stage to film close-ups. When she plays, Carole gets totally involved in her music. She seems not to hear or see anything going on around her.

Her last song was one of her best-known numbers, "You've Got a Friend," which she dedicated to her good friend and fellow rock star, James Taylor. As the applause finally died down, Carole walked swiftly off-stage through the crowd and disappeared into a waiting limousine. But the spirit of friendship and cooperation she'd engendered lingered on in Central Park. In a demonstration of good will, rare among audiences of any kind, Carole's fans accepted the garbage bags being handed out by park department workers and stayed after the concert to help pick up leftover debris. By midnight, all evidence of the event had vanished; and Central Park was quiet again.

Striving for Simplicity

My life has been a tapestry of rich and royal hue,
An everlasting vision of the everchanging view,
A wondrous, woven magic in bits of blue and gold,
A tapestry to feel and see, impossible to hold.

Many rock stars lead flamboyant lives. They wear loud clothes, make outlandish statements to the press, and enjoy all the publicity hugely. Carole King has rejected all that. She lives quietly with her second husband, bass player Charles Larkey, and four children near Los An-

geles, California. Her life centers around her family.

Even Carole's performances are a family affair. Her husband Charles shares her love of music. Ever since her first album, he has played bass on her records. He also tours with her as a member of the David T. Walker Band, which opens Carole's shows and also provides backup accompaniment for her.

Carole limits her concert tours so that she can spend most of her time with her children. Recently, she had a chance to write a number of songs especially for them. Some of the best-loved poems and stories of Maurice Sendak, a noted children's author, were being adapted for a television special, "Really, Rosie." Carole was asked to compose music for Sendak's poems and to sing the songs on television. On the night of the special, her own children, as well as thousands of others across the country, sat glued to their television sets, as Carole King's voice made Rosie, the brash little imp from Brooklyn, come alive.

Carole composes all the songs she sings on her records. She also does her own arrangements, and recently she's been writing her own lyrics too. Carole's songs, like her life, are focused on close relationships with other people. Her songs are almost always addressed to someone specific. She's always talking to a certain "you" out there, reaching out *to* someone.

"I have always written more in the direction of my friends and family," she says. "I like to touch them with my songs; touching a mass of people is a whole other trip — it is a high energy trip, and it's very exciting, but it's another trip."

Carole describes herself as a "contented homebody." She loves to cook — especially with natural foods. One of her specialties is Japanese-style raw fish. At recording sessions, Carole often brings out fresh home-baked cookies for the performers and studio technicians.

Carole tries to keep her life and her family's as simple and natural as possible. The Larkey's white frame home in Laurel Canyon is modest and unpretentious. Carole drives the children to school in a battered white Volkswagen. She prefers jeans to designer fashions and family picnics to cocktail parties. For relaxation, she does needlepoint and practices yoga. An enthusiastic advocate of natural childbirth, Carole had her fourth child at home.

Unlike many busy people, Carole takes time to appreciate life's simple pleasures — playing with her children, talking with friends, throwing a stick for her dog, stitching a needlepoint pillow, or just sitting still by a window, enjoying the warm spring sunshine on her face.

Carole's songs are made of the same stuff as her life. They contain a kind of magic which comes of being intensely aware of the potential of even life's ordinary moments. To Carole, even a mother's daily chore of getting breakfast on the table can be a suitable subject for a song.

Pieces of toast — raspberry jam
Laid out on the breakfast table—
It's time to begin again.

In her songs, as in her life, Carole strives for simplicity. She seems to be saying that the ordinary, everyday things most people overlook may be the most important of all.

Many critics have remarked that Carole King's songs always sound best when she sings them herself. As one reviewer put it, it's the "extra-musical dimension of her personality that makes her records so compelling." Carole's warm personality shines through in her music. When she sings, Carole doesn't hold anything back. Even on records she reaches out to an audience, openly revealing her feelings in a way few other singers do. Beneath the surface of her deceptively simple songs runs a subtle undercurrent of emotion. As one critic remarked, "The woman's got soul."

Song-writer

Carole King became a performer only recently — her first album *Carole King — Writer* was released in 1970. But she has been writing hit songs for 15 years. She actually got her start in the music business by responding to a challenge from a high school classmate.

Back in 1957, Carole King was a student at Madison High School in Brooklyn, New York. Among her friends was Neil Sedaka, who later became a well-known writer of popular songs. One of Neil's first hits was a song he wrote about Carole King called "Oh, Carol." When Carole heard the song, she immediately responded by writing a song about Sedaka called "Oh, Neil."

Although "Oh, Neil" never became a hit, Carole kept on writing songs. After she'd graduated from high school, she enrolled at Queens College in New York. But she dropped out of college in her freshman year to marry Gerry Goffin, a chemistry student who shared her interest in popular music.

In 1960, both Carole and Gerry signed a contract with Aldon Music, a new publishing firm. By then, rock 'n roll reigned supreme on the teenage music scene. Aldon's owners, Al Nevins and Donny Kirschner, figured there was big money to be made in publishing songs which would appeal especially to teen-agers. Most other firms published all kinds of music; but Nevins and Kirschner decided that Aldon Music would concentrate solely on the teenage market.

Aldon Music eventually employed over 30 of America's top songwriters. For a while, the company produced a large percentage of the country's popular music. Donny Kirschner, who became known as the "King of Bubble Gum Music," didn't care whether his songwriters created beautiful songs. He just wanted them to turn out a product which would sell. There was terrific pressure to produce hit songs.

The writers' work day started at 9:00 with everyone assembled for a conference. Donny Kirschner would tell them, "We need a smash hit for Bobby Vee." Then all the writers would go off into separate rooms with their paper and pencils. "We each had a little cubbyhole with just enough room for a piano, a bench, and maybe a chair for the lyricist — if you were lucky." Carole later recalled in an interview. "You'd sit there and write, and you could hear someone in the next cubbyhole composing some song exactly like yours." The next day, all the writers would audition for Bobby Vee's producer, who would choose the songs he liked.

Fortunately, Carole and Gerry Goffin worked well under this kind of pressure. They emerged as Aldon Music's most successful songwriting team. Because they were not much older than the teen-agers they were writing for, Carole and Gerry understood teen-agers' concerns. They were able to capture in their songs the way teenagers thought and felt. To their young audiences, their songs seemed to ring true.

The first Goffin-King hit was "Will You Love Me

Tomorrow?'' Recorded by a group called the Shirelles, the song hit the charts on November 27, 1960, and stayed on Billboard's ''Hot 100'' for 19 weeks, eventually climbing to number one. ''Will You Love Me Tomorrow?'' was different from most of the songs of the late 1950's which tended to be rather trite.

Compared to most songs of the time, ''Will You Love Me Tomorrow'' was refreshingly realistic: ''Tonight with words unspoken/You say that I'm the only one/But will my heart be broken/When the night meets the morning sun?'' Most of Carole and Gerry's best songs were similar to this — simple but poignant, sentimental but not overly so.

Carole and Gerry wrote many songs for black vocal groups such as the *Drifters,* the *Crystals,* and the *Ronettes.* Many of these songs were written in a style known as ''Uptown Rhythm and Blues'' — music which had something of the feel of traditional black music but was directed at the white teenage audience which bought most of the single records.

Like most ''Uptown R & B'' the Goffin-King version was popular music with a blues feel. It was music of the city, rather than the country. One of the best Goffin-King songs, ''Up on the Roof,'' is about city people's need to escape from the noise and crowds of the city's busy streets and find a quiet place to be alone — even if it's only ''up on the roof.'' The song first became a hit for the *Drifters* in 1962. Carole herself later recorded it on her first album in 1970.

Gerry Goffin and Carole King also wrote songs for specific solo artists, both black and white. Their biggest success was with Bobby Vee, for whom they wrote a number of hit songs, including ''Take Good Care of My

Baby," "Walkin' With My Angel," and "I Can't Say Goodbye." Aretha Franklin and Steve Lawrence also had big hits with their songs.

Carole and Gerry discovered one performer who successfully recorded their songs. When they found their maid had a powerful voice, they persuaded her to record one of their novelty songs called "Loco-motion." The song became a hit; and their maid, billed as "Little Eva," found a new career as a singer.

Carole and Gerry seemd to be able to write songs that conveyed the particular "sound" any artist or group specialized in. On the other hand, their songs were curiously adaptable. Many of them could be performed successfully in any number of different styles.

In 1962, Steve Lawrence had a hit with "Go Away Little Girl," sung in an "easy-listening" manner. Eleven years later Donny Osmond revived the same song, sung very differently as a teenage lament at frustrated love. In between, Count Basie gave it a jazzy treatment, and Lawrence Welk recorded it as pure pop. Since the Shirelles first recorded "Will You Love Me Tomorrow?" in 1960, the song has been recorded by no fewer than 54 different artists and groups, from Pat Boone to Roberta Flack. Carole herself recorded it recently.

The early 60's were golden years for Carole King. Almost every song she and Gerry Goffin wrote seemed to become a hit. But in the mid 1960's, the Beatles and other British rock groups burst onto the popular music scene. The new groups changed more than the kind of music that was played — they caused a revolution in the music-publishing business as well. The Beatles, Bob Dylan, and other groups and artists on the rise in the mid 60's didn't depend on professional songwriters for their material.

They preferred to write their own songs. It became harder and harder for Carole King and other songwriters to find topflight artists to record their songs.

Finding the market for his writers' songs had dried up, Carole's boss, Donny Kirschner, decided to form his own groups to sing his writers' songs. By then, Aldon Music had been sold to Columbia Pictures. Columbia TV created the "Monkees," a new situation comedy for children. Carole King and Gerry Goffin were asked to write some of the music for the show, but it wasn't a great success.

Goin' Back

I think I'm goin' back
To the things I learned so well
in my youth.
I think I'm returning to
Those days when I was young
enough to know the truth.

Carole and Gerry Goffin found that it was difficult to maintain a marriage, working together under pressure every day at Aldon Music. It had been bad enough during the good years when almost all their songs were hits; But as fewer and fewer of their songs were accepted by producers, the strain became even greater.

Because of their personal problems, in the mid-60's, Carole and Gerry began to have trouble writing music together. During this period only three of their songs, "Natural Woman," "Goin' Back," and "Wasn't Born to Follow," became big hits.

These songs were very different from the ones they'd written earlier. Possibly because they were older, Carole and Gerry no longer seemed to be able to write the teenage love songs which had provided most of their earlier hits. Their music became more thoughtful and troubled, probably reflecting both their failing marriage and the problems they could see in society.

During the mid-60's, the entire country was increasingly troubled and divided by the war in Vietnam, by the assassination of three of its most respected leaders, by student protests and civil rights demonstrations. Two of the three hit songs Carole and Gerry Goffin wrote during this period reflected their concern about these problems. In "Goin' Back," they seemed to be saying that with the future so uncertain, the only way to be happy is to try to go back to the past. In "Wasn't Born to Follow," they pictured life as a journey, with the traveler uncertain which way to go.

During the middle 60's Carole and Gerry's songs were recorded by different types of artists than those who'd recorded their previous material. "Natural Woman" was a hit for Aretha Franklin in the new "soul" field. A rock group called *The Byrds* sang "Wasn't Born to Follow" on the sound track of *Easy Rider,* a movie highly critical of American society and its values.

The Byrds also recorded "Goin' Back," one of the last hit songs Carole and Gerry wrote together. In 1968, the Goffins ended both their songwriting partnership and their marriage. Carole King moved to the West Coast with her two daughters, determined to build a new life on her own and "get together a new identity."

Singer

Ever since she first started writing for Aldon Music in the 50's, Carole King had played the piano and sung on demos for other singers. Many of her friends told her she ought to make records herself. Don Everly, of the Everly Brothers, once told an interviewer that he'd saved all the tapes she'd made for him. "They always sounded better to me than the final versions of the songs," he said. Other singers felt the same way and also collected Carole King demos.

In 1961, Carole persuaded Don Kirschner to let her audition with one of her own songs. "It Might As Well Rain Till September" was released as a single in 1962 on Kirschner's Dimension label. It remained on the best-selling record charts for nine weeks, climbing to #22 on Billboard's "Hot 100" chart in the United States and reaching the #1 spot in Great Britain.

But in spite of her success with "It Might As Well Rain Until September," Carole went back to her writing. Except for demos, she didn't do any more recording until after her break with Gerry Goffin. Then, in Los Angeles, Carole began singing and playing the piano with a group called *The City.* In 1969 she and the group did an album called *Now That Everything's Been Said,* using many of her old songs. The album was not successful, but it helped increase Carole's confidence in her singing.

The guitarist for *The City,* Danny Kootch, introduced Carole to rock star James Taylor, who had also recently come to Los Angeles from New York. Taylor asked Carole to play the piano on his album, *Sweet Baby James.* She began performing with Taylor, playing the piano for him and also singing on her own. James encouraged Carole to ask record producer, Lou Adler, to help her cut a solo album.

Lou Adler had started out in the publishing business and had later founded a record company, Ode Records. He had discovered a number of successful groups, among them, *The Mamas and The Papas.* Carole had known Adler for many years, and he had often encouraged her to record some of her songs. But when she approached him about doing a solo album, he was busy with other groups; so he referred her to a friend, John Fischbach, who produced her first album, *Carole King — Writer.*

The album contained twelve songs, many of them old Goffin-King favorites, such as, "Goin' Back," "Up On the Roof," and "No Easy Way Down." Almost all the songs had been recorded previously by other artists; but when Carole sang them, it was hard to recall the other versions, hers seemed so right.

Music critics were enchanted with the album. One reviewer raved: "Her music has the yeast and the vigor of rock, the impeccable good taste of jazz, and the subtlety of folk music — her songs are urban poetry — and her voice is that of a friend — comfortable, wise, kind, and easy to be with."

The album sold only 8,000 copies, mostly to friends of Carole's in the music business who had heard her demos over the years and were already fans of hers. But the album's slow sales didn't discourage Carole's friend, Lou Adler. He thought the album had great promise and immediately made plans to oversee the production of Carole's next solo album himself.

Six months later *Tapestry* was released. The album contained some songs Carole had written years before with Gerry Goffin, including their first hit, "Will You Love Me Tomorrow?" and "Natural Woman." There were also two songs Carole had written with Toni Stern, a friend from

Aldon Music; But over half the songs were ones Carole had written entirely herself. Some of these were among the best on the album — "I Feel the Earth Move," "So Far Away," and "You've Got a Friend."

Tapestry was a personal statement, an expression of an individual point of view. Back at Aldon Music, Carole had written songs for all sorts of other people and had become very good at expressing their personal styles. Now at last, she was writing for herself and singing her songs in her own way. Even the old Goffin-King songs which she included on the album were carefully chosen to express her own personal point of view. Carole ended the album with "Natural Woman," singing "Now I'm no longer doubtful of what I'm living for" with such conviction, it was impossible not to feel she meant it.

An intensity of feeling ran through Carole's *Tapestry* album. Her attitude toward life had changed since the days when she and Gerry were writing teenage love songs. She had suffered the pain of separation and divorce and the exhilarating but frightening experience of moving 3,000 miles from home to start a new life on her own. There had been lonely days and nights and moments of despair; But at last she was making it — not as an adjunct to someone else — but completely on her own, as a person and as a woman.

The songs on Carole's *Tapestry* album reflect a new, more mature point of view. Even in an exuberant love song like "I Feel the Earth Move" there is a suggestion that this is not the feeling of falling in love for the first time, but an ecstasy that comes from the painful awareness that love may not last forever.

The arrangements of the *Tapestry* songs were simple, almost spare. Carole sang some songs with piano only, or with piano and string bass accompaniment; But the simple

style enabled the emotional power of the music to come through. It worked.

Tapestry was a personal statement of rare eloquence and beauty; But the feelings Carole King expressed were also ones many other people could relate to. Rock fans and classical music buffs, college students and middle-aged couples who had hummed her earlier songs, all bought *Tapestry.* By 1973, the album had sold over 10 million copies, surpassing the sales of every other rock album and even such all-time top hits as *The Sound of Music.*

In Concert

After listening to her *Tapestry* album, many people were eager to hear Carole King in person. She was besieged with offers for concerts.

At first, Carole said she was not interested. She said that the only reason she had gotten into recording at all, was that she felt this was the fastest way to expose her songs to the public. Even after she began making records, she still considered herself basically a songwriter rather than a performer. "I want to play music," she said, "but I have no particular desire for the limelight itself. . . . I don't want to be a Star with a capital S."

However, in 1971, with her *Tapestry* album at the top of the charts, Carole reluctantly agreed to do a few solo concerts. Before, she had always performed with James Taylor, playing the piano for him, joining him for a few songs, then doing a few numbers on her own. James had helped her conquer the gripping fear she always felt when she performed in public. He had helped her learn to relax and be herself on stage.

Carole was almost paralyzed with fear at the thought of appearing on stage alone without James. She worried that the audience wouldn't respond — that the critics wouldn't like her songs — that she'd forget the words. But she felt it was important to try to conquer her stage fright. She felt that, in a way, to remain just a songwriter would be taking the easy way out. "As a writer, it's very safe and womb-like," she admitted. "Someone else gets the credit or the blame." So she agreed to try a solo concert.

Before her solo debut at the Troubador Club in Los Angeles, Carole worked out her whole act carefully in her mind. Again and again she went over exactly what she was going to do and say; But on May 18, 1971, the night of the concert, as she looked out over the audience, Carole felt the old fear engulfing her. Somehow she managed to start singing the first number. Then, suddenly, everything was all right. She was lost in the song, her nervousness forgotten.

After Carole's third number, a voice suddenly came over a loud speaker. Carole had a terrible sinking feeling that the person was going to tell her the act was awful and she had to get off the stage. But instead, the voice said, "Carole, you're not going to believe this, but there's been a rumor that there is a bomb in the Troubador." Despite the seriousness of the situation, Carole had only a feeling of relief that the problem was something other than her singing. She told the audience that; and they laughed, breaking the tension.

No bomb was found. Carole went on with the show, relaxed now and more comfortable than she'd ever expected to feel. "I realized that a stage is, after all, a stage," she said later, "and I am here to do a show. All I have to do is just be myself and do whatever it is I do, and that seems to work out OK."

After the Troubador concert, Carole was asked to perform in Carnegie Hall, an invitation which has always symbolized success for popular singers as well as symphony musicians. Some people expected Carole to develop a routine or at least to polish her act a bit for the big event. But even at Carnegie Hall, Carole was determined just to be herself.

On the night of the concert, June 18, 1971, she came out in a simple print dress and sat down at the piano. Then she looked out at the standing-room-only audience which overflowed the main floor and all four of the ornate old balconies, and said merely, "Hello." Carole's simplicity and lack of pretentiousness set the mood for the evening. Her warmth and friendliness won the audience over completely before she'd even begun to sing.

Carole did two shows that night at Carnegie Hall. By the end of the second show, her voice was tired; but the excitement was still there. The audience felt it too. One critic said afterwards that as a singer, "she lends her soulful melodies the kind of definitive style which can only be called greatness."

A few weeks after the Carnegie Hall concert, Carole gave a concert at London's Festival Hall. The English audiences were equally enthusiastic. One reviewer said, "Carole King, sitting at the piano with her unique repertoire, was a new experience for us all, and quite simply electric." Another critic wrote, "Somehow, the popular music of ten years was embodied in Carole's all-too-short time on stage. At the Festival Hall she established herself as the First Lady of popular song."

After returning from England, Carole set out on a 35-day tour of the United States with James Taylor. The audiences were enthusiastic, but being on the road was terribly tiring for Carole. She found it difficult to do the same show night after night and still retain the freshness and spontaneity audiences had come to expect of her. "When you start singing a song, you just get lost in the song; and the fact that you've done it before doesn't really matter," she said. ". . . It's just that I don't like the part between numbers."

Carole also found that she was doing so much performing, she didn't have time to do what she felt she did best — write songs. "I'm not that great a singer," she said. "The thing that I have to get to the people — the thing I'm performing for — are the songs. . . . I would rather just go and devote all my energy to writing new songs so I can give that to people."

Being on the road so much also made Carole feel uneasy about her family. Her new husband, bass player, Charles Larkey, traveled with her. But she felt she was away from her daughters too much. Then in the middle of her 1971 tour, Carole found she was pregnant. She cancelled the remaining concerts on the tour and went home to California. Carole decided that from then on, she would concentrate on recording her songs rather than giving concerts. She realized that a record wasn't quite as satisfactory for an audience as a live performance, but she felt she needed more time to write and more time for her family.

To the surprise and dismay of her many fans, in mid-1971 Carole King abruptly disappeared from the concert scene. A month before her baby was due, she finished work on her third album, *Carole King — Music.* But even after the baby was born, she did not schedule any more personal appearances.

In March, 1972, the record industry announced its choices for the top records and performers of the year

Carole King was awarded four Grammys. She won the awards for: Record of the Year, "It's Too Late"; Album of the Year, *Tapestry;* Song of the Year, "You've Got a Friend"; and Best Female Pop Vocal Performance, *Tapestry.* In 1972, the Grammy Awards were to be presented for the first time on a live television show; But Carole King, the only performer to win more than one award, did not come to the ceremony. She told reporters that she regretted not being able to attend, but she was still nursing her baby and felt she could not leave home.

Even though she was busy with her new baby, Carole found time to write the songs for her *Rhymes and Reasons* album, released in 1972. During all of that year, however, Carole gave only two concerts — both benefits for Senator George McGovern's presidential campaign.

In 1973, when she finished work on her *Fantasy* album, she agreed to make a 12-city tour to introduce her new songs. The first concert was scheduled for Central Park in New York City. Carole purposely chose to return to New York to start her tour. "There's something about returning to your home town," she told friends. ". . . even if your home town happens to be the biggest city in the world. New York has given me such an awful lot — stimulus, ideas, feelings to write. . . . The concert is just a small way of giving something back to it."

Critical reaction to the albums Carole did after *Tapestry* had been less than enthusiastic. Reaction to her *Fantasy* album was specially negative. Reviewers said the album was monotonous and preachy. In the songs on this album, Carole wrote for the first time, not about personal relationships, but about problems in society — dangers of drug addiction; need for equality between black and white people, men and women; and the need for human understanding. The new approach didn't seem to work. Carole was at her best writing intimate songs addressed to one specific person, rather than delivering a pronouncement on the ills of society.

But even Carole's less-than-perfect songs were exciting when she sang them in a live performance. In concert, the air of solemnity felt on the record disappeared. After a London concert, a reviewer reported that Carole performed "Corazon" with such energy and enthusiasm she almost had the audience bopping in the aisles.

Carole remains philosophical about both praise and criticism, success and failure. She thinks timing had a lot to do with her success with *Tapestry.* "It's a question of everything moving in cycles," she says. "People got sick of the psychedelic sound and wanted softer moods."

If and when popular taste again shifts away from her kind of music and on to something else, Carole will not be overly upset. If no one else is interested, she'll go back to writing and singing for her family and friends. In any case, she won't try to relive her old successes.

With the current nostalgia craze, radio stations have recently revived many of her old songs. Carole has enjoyed hearing the originals of some of her big 60's hits on the radio. But she finds it disturbing when new groups try to recreate that old sound. "They're not moving forward, they're just capitalizing on sentimentality," she says. "It's kind of sad. That period's over."

Carole intends to keep on exploring new ideas and new sounds. She says it best in one of her songs:

Music is playing inside my head
Over and over and over again.
My friend, there's no end to the music.

JACKSON FIVE
CARLY SIMON
BOB DYLAN
JOHN DENVER
THE BEATLES
ELVIS PRESLEY
JOHNNY CASH
CHARLEY PRIDE
ARETHA FRANKLIN
ROBERTA FLACK
STEVIE WONDER
NEIL DIAMOND
CAROLE KING
DIANA ROSS
THE OSMONDS
CHARLIE RICH
ELTON JOHN
CHICAGO
FRANK SINATRA
BARBRA STREISAND
OLIVIA NEWTON-JOHN